Wondering
and
Wandering

Wondering
and
Wandering

Poems from Dharamshala

PRAHLAD SHEKHAWAT

PARTRIDGE

To order additional copies of this book, contact
Partridge India
000 800 10062 62
orders.india@partridgepublishing.com

www.partridgepublishing.com/india

Contents

Foreword and Introduction...........................7

Lost Beat 21
The New Moon..............................23
Kangra Valley to Triund..................27
The Old Trail.............................. 31
First Light 35
Main Square 39
Nomads, Pilgrims and Tradesman 43
Many Types in Dharamshala................49
Angles of Views 53
The Church in the Wilderness 57
Traveller 61
Mind's Breath Travelling.................65
Wandering with the Breath................69
Window Tree...............................73
Solitude and Loneliness..................77
Fellow Traveller.........................79
Two birds and Joy 81
No Message is Found......................85
A Beggar Woman's Blessings 87
An American Nun friend................... 91
Holy and Romantic Man....................95
A Romantic Holy Man......................97
Too Much Snow & Too Little Water 99
Mountain Witness........................ 103
My India 107

Foreword and Introduction

These poems are based on my many sojourns to Dharamshala nearly every summer for so many years. I have seen Dharamshala change from when it a was sleepy town with the main square was occupied by one bus coming and going in the morning and one in the evening and for the rest it was like a parking place for sheep and goats on transit to greener pastures. The first wave of tourists mostly Western people started pouring in after His Holiness the Dalai Lama won the Nobel Peace Prize and became a world icon for peace and compassion. His persona attracted many who were charmed by his ideas and personality so much that many of them decided to stay and become practicing Buddhists. It is not surprising that Buddhism is now one of the fasted spreading faiths, at least in the Western world, if not elsewhere as well.

The closure or partial closure of Kashmir due to the trouble there lead to a large influx of mainly Indian tourists to seek cool chimes in Dharamshala which then became a popular hill station as the British had imagined it to be so many years ago during the colonial era. The Church in the Wilderness bears testimony to the bygone era by displaying the cracks it sustained during a severe earthquake which destroyed the British

Raj's dream of setting up Dharamshala as the summer capital of the colonial rule. The Church in Wilderness's yard is filled with fallen heroes of the Raj who died due to dysentery or other tropical diseases including snake bite etc.

The third wave of tourist influx was triggered by the advent of cricket after the start of the IPL or the Indian Premium League devoted to cricket matches being played at one of the most spectacular cricket grounds anywhere with the backdrop of the Dauladhar Mountains looming large in a striking manner. This backdrop provided such a beautiful view enticing so many who were lured by the television images to seek out Dharamshala which otherwise and probably for good would have remained a much quieter place. This new influx also included a large number of young people who in their big and loud cars came to gaze at their stars who had become cricket celebrities and who waived to them from high up standing on their hotel balconies.

The other reason for the popularity of Dharamshala is based on its lying along the route or near some of the famous Hindu and Buddhist ancient shrines which traverse the length and breadth of the Himalayas lying in this particular stretch. The pilgrims also like to visit the nearby shrine of Bhagsu Nag which is a Shiva temple next to an ice cool stream pouring into what is now a popular swimming pool. The waterfall a little further up provides a picnic spot and the walk up to it is wonderful especially the walk to the waterfall and the cafe above from the upper route, which is away from the traffic jams and the crowds below. The traffic jams mainly in Bhagsu Nag and at the main square in Mcleod Ganj are hard to imagine in what once was a serene and quite place with hardly any cars. The easy availability of loan to buy a car by nearly any one and the growing culture of EMI's or easy monthly payments. Such a culture was possible with the rise of the middle and lower middle class in India which has spiralled into a massive rise in car ownership, making the country the second largest market for cars and recently growing number of big cars, after China. The cars not only cause traffic jams and pollution but also spoil the serene and spiritual atmosphere of the place which is supposed to be spiritual place and a sight of pilgrimage.

One had suggested that the main roads in Mcleod Ganj and even the one leading to Bhagsu Nag could be made traffic and car free except the plying of a electric small bus to ferry people who are unable to walk or prefer a mode of transparent which is pollution and noise free and does not create the havoc and chaos leading to heated arguments and fights that has become characteristic of the town for some time now. One hopes that like other hill stations such as Nainital in Uttar Pradesh and Musourie in Uttrakhand and Shimla in Himachal Pradesh itself, Mcleod Ganj or

Upper Dharamshala ought to become traffic and car free zone where supplies can be delivered at certain times of the day without any problem, thereby posing a threat to the environment and to the serenity of the town in such a brutal and aggressive way as it seems to have become now.

My poems bemoan the loss of those earlier quiet and pristine times when being a traveller meant walking through the streets paved with cobbled stones along with the sheep and goats and villagers with their traditional clothes with a rope tied around their waste and the women in the sliver finery which reminded me of my native Rajasthan. Over the years I became more of a mountain person and in some ways a kind of a nomad like the Gaddi people who used to travel with their sheep and goats to lower or upper regions with the change of seasons.

These Gaddis who are classified as tribes have a rich cultural heritage and deserve a place to preserve and celebrate their heritage like a museum and cultural centre which one has been trying to help establish without too much success. Hopefully soon this will be possible with the support and cooperation of the local people among whom are some of my good friends.

The Tibetan refugee population has been trickling in consistently although recently they have dwindled in numbers as the Chinese have imposed restrictions. Many Tibetans send their children to study in the well endowed and famous Tibetan Children Village School, not far with its own play ground and well constructed housing complex. Recently with the arrival of the Karmapa and other religiously famous people more Westerners and other devotees have started coming, although the Karmapa lives in his grand monastery outside the Dharamshala area, which makes the devotee population more dispersed in other parts of the Kangra region and also along the border of Palampur which is another city nearby.

The Idea of this book came from my own experiences and ideas of imaginative flights while living and moving around in Dharamshala and its surrounding areas which were both interesting and amazingly beautiful as long as I could get away from the traffic and one could view the panoramic views without the hindrance of the crowds and the glare of city's noise and pollution. Dharamshala can be interesting also because it does not allow for too many unnecessary distractions except those presented by nature and the cultural artefacts to be found in some place of historic interest like the Bhagsu Nag temple.

This temple was designed to withstand earthquakes which the British forgot to do by not building many areas of support and corridors to withstand shocks which one can see in Bhagsu Nag. The sheer range of natural places around and the natural landscape around the town is laudable. However one is not able to say the same about the main roads and the normal street life which is full of turmoil and chaos and which has now unfortunately become the mainstay of life in Dharamshala or to be precise of upper Dharamshala.

In case there is any doubt about Dhramshala's natural beauty one should go up to Triund and watch the glacier beyond, which alas I did not have the fortune to visit but I am told by reliable sources that the glacier is sliding down and the snow and ice melt recently was heavy and the anecdotal evidence for the warming of the globe and for Climate Change is mounting. This is so even if there are no data which had been studied systematically for this region. However the heavy snow cover I saw the other summer was astounding and the village lady in Upper Dharamshala told me that that year the crop had to be cut early as the sowing season had already begun because the rains had come early and the crop had to be cut prematurely to make way for the next round of crop.

This situation is further worsened by the growing stress that tourism is placing on the local resources, places and agricultural cycle by the encroachment on the arable land which then tends to be used for construction of hotels and guest houses indiscriminately for the tourists who are unmindful and careless of their impact on the local economy which is growing year by year. However the impact in the long run is likely to lead to the paucity of grain and fodder for animals made from the stumps and leftovers after the crop has been cut. The growing local economy may not deliver because tourism may decline if the Indian political and economic system itself may do so as the trends could perhaps be foreseen if they are properly analysed in terms of their environmental viability and the large ecological footprint that the new lifestyle is likely to carry. Apart from that there are social and cultural factors which create a climate of fear and suspicion such as the increase in crime and sexual abuse including that of foreign tourists.

Therefore the many sided advances in the economy may not make the local people happy nor bring the benefits expected from such tourist development. Already there are signs that many of such developments make people restless and lead to loss of cultural heritage and the sense of belonging and community which traditionally was enjoyed by the locals like the Gaddis who would live in close knit communities with a Goddess of the mountains akin to Durga presiding as the deity to protect them from calamites and bring good fortune to them.

These developments are not unique and do not portend the downfall of the local people as they are hardy with much resilience and with the added benefit of the profits they receive from the recent knowledge that their lands are being restored to them in a collective and equal manner unlike in the case of the other communities which are caste ridden, because the Gaddis are now legally classified as a tribe. However even among the Gaddis as well, the caste has raised its ugly head and the society is not without its issues of caste consciousness and some discrimination due the rising social divisions which include some well off higher caste on the one hand and the poorer so called lower caste. This is unfortunately the new trend although traditionally as a tribal people the Gaddis are did not believe in the caste system.

The Gaddis had affiliation with the tribal people across the Tibetan border now marked by Chinese flags, where they travelled not only for grazing their herds but also to trade in salt, silk and other commodities and therefore could be considered part of the silk route. Such routes have now been closed and have been replaced by semi automatic guns and flags of nations instead of prayer and peace flags normally to be seen. One can sometimes see these peace and prayer flags in Dharamshala at crossroads between one path and the other moving zigzag in converse directions.

The pattern of life of these Gaddi people should be a matter of pride for us but for the fact that they do not enjoy the patronage of the tourists as the Tibetans do, leading to resentment and envy as the Tibetans tended to corner most of the business until recently when the Gaddis and the local Pahadis, Panjabis and the Thakurs moved in to take advantage of growing tourist business and are now playing a much more active role. Such a role may not fit in with the keen sense of rivalry one sees among the Gaddis who vie with each other to capture the business.

The gentle ways and polite customs of the Tibetan people contrasts strangely with the aggressive and loud Punjabi mainstream culture from the plains flooding in which mainly consist of young people who tax the local Indian people like the Gaddis who are not able to identify with them. The Tibetans provide the Punjabis from the plains with accommodation and food with the possibility that they can be reformed but the loud mouthed Punjabis and their rabid ways are not easy to change. Punjabis are quite happy to ride in their big and loud cars with blazing horns, unmindful of the sanctity of a spiritual and serene place which Dharamshala is supposed to be.

This raises the question as to what should be the role of a poet and writer who cannot have much influence over the course of the events except to raise some pertinent issues, hopefuly, and to make some protestations and raise the voice of those who fervently wish for change. One met an older couple who recently moved to Aurovillle international community near Poduherry in South India, after living in Dharamshala for some years when they realised that they could not stop the place from being taken over by commence and encroachments by loud Israeli youth and even louder

Punjabi young people. Both of these have managed to change the character of the serene and quiet hamlet which Dharamkot in Upper Dharamshala used to be; with its many gentle local people, mules and sheep and the refined monks of the Tushita Monastery and the earnest devotees and students from the Vipassna Centre nearby.

Dharamkot now has become a sort of a Yoga capital with many centres or Yoga shops sprouting up with their part time teachers who manage to make a living by teaching Yoga. Many a times these teaches also try to seek foreign girl friends whom they flaunt instead of making it a more modest affair by keeping in mind the sanctity of the place and keeping in mind the feelings and dignity of the local people who may think it all as a sort of fair game. The local people may not realise that their idea of making friends and girl friends may not work in many cases and may actually lead to frustration and disillusionment.

It seems the social fabric of the place is not changing for the better and may in some way be heading for some troubling times as wealth increases as do expectations with no equivalent increase in satisfaction levels. People seem to be making a big effort to make a mockery of their relationships in different ways and manage to seek laurels in terms of how many girls one can catch. What is more important becomes secondary, which ought to be the seeking of love, genuine emotions and true attachment with the person one is associated with.

One has been part of the scene in some way and seen through it while at the same time fallen prey to its charms yet still managing to salvage oneself from its clutches to search for other more higher ideals and pursuits or at least that is what one hoped; pursuits like taking walks in nature, having a quite time with oneself and making friends who may not be useful in any other way except that they are simply friends for their own sake, regardless of gender.

One also tried to make some sense of the Buddhist ideas of compassion and wisdom and did courses at the Tibetan Library and the Tushita Monastery. I also interviewed His Holiness the Dalai Lama who taught me not to be so complacent about knowing the seminal ideas of Buddhism and look deeper for the ideas related to reincarnation and rebirth which I now do and think they are more related to moments of significant change as the Venerable Thik Nach Hanh, who is a Vietnamese Monk living in France, says: every new moment is like a rebirth and every day one rises to greet is like a rebirth.

What makes Dharamshala special for me is the range of activities and things to do which does not require much money and which makes it a less challenging place for people who may be older in age, others of all ages and denominations and for those who cannot afford too much to spend. These activities include walking in nature as I said and also making many friends who become part of one's life in a strange way which is a kind of a healthy way of being in a place which does not belong to one's birth but is still part of one's being in a sort of roundabout way, as I realised during my stay in this extra ordinary place.

What then gives a place its sense of belonging is difficult to define but the place must make us feel at home and comfortable without losing our sense of authentic orientation and cultural moorings even if they happen to be those of what someone has called "Desi Cosmopolitanism"; "Desi" meaning indigenous or local. That is what makes a place worth living at and belonging to, or at least these are some of the elements that make it worthwhile to belong somewhere. One can say one has lived in a place when one has lived there all the four seasons, has some good friends there and when one can pick up some of the local tongue. Only then one can say that one has rightfully lived in that place, as someone has noted. I have done all these except living here in the middle of the winter which maybe cold but maybe nice without the traffic and the jostling crowds which could make the summer experience worth avoiding.

I hope I can come to live in Dharamshala during the winter when the life is quieter and make it my home place where the sunrise is as interesting as the sunset and where the glowing of the light makes one's heart warm truly kind and compassionate; knowing that one is not alone in sharing the warmth of the place and there are others who also shiver in the cold and there are others that manage without proper heating and without hot shower.

One hopes one is able to make the writing of poetry memorable by reflecting the mood of the place and which then make it worth visiting it again with a new perspective in order to make it look as if one is discovering the place for the first time. As the poet T S Eliot opined wisely: after making all the voyages and travelling around the world, the main point is to come back and look at the place from where one started with fresh eyes so that it becomes another voyage of discovery.

Prahlad Shekhawat

Lost Beat

The Dhauladhar mountain
Echoing
with the monsoon raga,
said to me:
I cannot fathom
the endless journeys
and
yearnings of your heart
In the thunder,
lightning
and
swirling clouds,
That are wrapped
around me.
I will play
the cosmic orchestra
To rhyme
With
your out of tune
heart
That has journeyed
back,
In search of
its lost beat
Longing
to hear
its own
echo

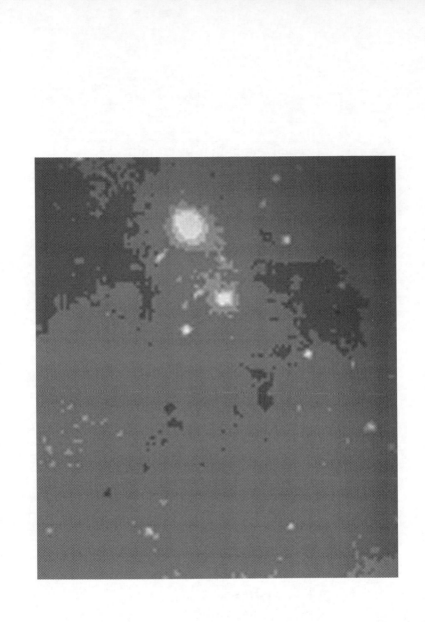

The New Moon

Just when I looked
up
appeared
the new moon
Perched
on extended branch
of mountain slopes,
Suddenly
it is transformed
into floating specs
of clouds.

Then its feathers ruffled,
a white
dancing dove unfurling.
Is the crescent
holding Shiva's hair
like a pin,
or
Is it holding
the mosque I saw
on the way up from Patahnkot
by its dome,

Prahlad Shekhawat

or like
on the main square
the Tibetan monastery
with its Ashoka's Wheel
of Dharma,
above it
the brass spires
being framed
like a flower mist
Christmas decoration,
The crowning glory
Is the new moon
a sign
or symbol?

Prahlad Shekhawat

Kangra Valley to Triund

The hot dusty plains
of Punjab
Skirting
the border posts
of Pakistan
roll
into the tropical green
of Kangra,
With
its sloping tea gardens
studded
with mango trees
Little
girls with pony tails
march
unescorted
up and down
the hill
to school
The flat
rivers flow faster
as waterfalls

The road
curls up straight as
the khadi dandi;
the path like a straight stick
up into
the pine forest
along the Church
in the Wilderness,
that is
If
you can escape
the traffic jam
Beyond
the Shiva temple
with the glacial spring
lies the Bagsu river,
Weaving
Through the pebbles and rocks
and drying
monk's red robes
Now
snaking up
in whirlpools
then a falling
sheet of water,
And further up
suspended pools
in the boulders.

The trek
to Triund
leaves behind
pine and foliage
Criss-crossing
the meditation junction,
of the Tushita Monastery
and the Vipassana Centre
The young Westerners
with yoga mats,
And the terrace fields
of Dharamkot.
The barren stretch
is almost empty
with its dry tongue
Licking
the snow line.
Beyond
the horizon
the patchwork
of white-black
snowy peaks
and the Indira Pass
lies
another valley,
with
its own unfolding
cultural fables
and
Eco-tales

Prahlad Shekhawat

The Old Trail

There is a trail
from
upper Bagsu
to Shiva Cafe,
Above the waterfall
away
from the lower regions,
It is
almost forgotten,
civilised people
take
the cement road,
Down and up along
the river,
red
with drying
monks robes.
Old trails
have their purpose,
crows and eagles
know that

The crow
flies straight,
as they say:
straight as the crow flies,
the eagle
up and up around
in thermal circles.
A grazing route,
a quiet walk
in the wilderness,
From one view
to another angle,
shifting horizons,
Connections are made
with
unfolding
folds of the valleys,
One can
find God
in every stone,
hidden message
in every breeze,
The nearly and
bare mountain
with cascading
stones of slate,
Whose sun mica
surface glows
like quick silver:

Another shimmering
waterfall
of slate
and light,
Is framed
by the branches
of a mixed forest,
The songs
of birds,
the loud crackling
of crickets
and the sound
of silence
All separate,
still blend
in the wind flow,
with one's
deep breathing.
One
rests in the cool shade
against the pine tree,
inhaling the panorama,
A traveller
catching her or his
breath
Between
one watering hole
and another.

Prahlad Shekhawat

First Light

The peak
peeped through
the straddling valleys
Its eyes heavy
with fresh snow,
The pine row
framing the silhouette,
In the early twilight
Overlapping
moonset and sunrise

In the folds
of the breathing
and awakening
earth,
In the
no man's land
between
the bare slopes
and
the snow line,
mingled
with the perfume
of the pine fur

the smoke signal
of clouds rise
as if
a flame is lit
from
an unknown source
beyond,
a light
is caught
by
the slate and stone
getting bright
brand new and sharp

Main Square

Long time ago
in the main square,
no cars
Only a parking place
for sheep and goats,
on the way
from high passes
to low grazing slopes.
Only one bus
in the morning,
one in the evening.

Before Dalai Lama ji
got the Nobel Prize
when Kashmir bound tourists
were diverted this way.
Before
the IPL cricket matches
brought star gazing
crowds from the plains.
Choking breath
And choked view
Traffic jams
jam one's spirit.

Big brooding mountains
Watch:
quiet witness to history
The air is not at peace.
The corner pine tree
is half black,
The eagle
on its bare branch
castes a weary eye
on the
overbuilt ridge.

Nomads, Pilgrims and Tradesman

The Gaddi
Tribal man showed me
from
the mountain top
near the temple of the Goddess
a form of Durga
The junction of
grazing routes
of sheep and goats,
holding a water tank
and many winding paths
zig zag, up and down.
One path leads
up beyond the highest path
to the land of
the Yogi Lamas

If you carry on further
over the snow line
and vast stretches
of empty land,
which know
no
national boundaries,
only
endless boundless land
of ecology and paths
trodden by nomads, their animals,
by tradesman of spices and salt
by pilgrims with their beads,
faith wrapped around
like a shawl.

The Gaddi Tribals
also took
one of these paths
to Mount Kailash
to the glistening
shimmering waters
of Mansarovar
to their Tribal kinsmen
in another holy land,
the abode of Shiva,
their Adidevta;
the divine being since
the beginning of time.

These paths lie broken,
divided by
national frontiers,
Guarded by
national flags
not flags of prayer
and peace
The Tribal's divinity of
mountains and lakes
are now frequented
by
Tourists
with sun cream
and credit cards,
charged in juan
and green dollars bills

The new tradesman
has taken over
the nomad's
and pilgrim's paths
and the sacred space
of protector of forests
Shiva,
its creatures and the wild,
since beginning of time
It is now under border
control
Another dragon Calendar marks
the new time.

Prahlad Shekhawat

Many Types in Dharamshala

The German woman
finds Peace
in the mountains,
living simply
with the rhythm
of nature,
the French finds it
with the high lama,
and early morning
chanting.
Some travellers
cannot choose
between sex
and charas,
Both
mind altering substances

Another is caught
between Acrobatic Yoga
and Yoga
of mind acrobatics,
between vision and
breathing meditation.
One Indian teacher
thinks yoga
is the best posture
for buying a passage abroad.
One chose
voluntary work,
to teach
refugee children

In the cosy comfort of
a travellers haven,
Trying to pay back
debts to his conscience,
and have
his Bagsu cake too
So many types
in one
Indian place
called Dharmashala or
a refuge for a weary
pilgrim.

Angles of Views

The students
prostrate three times,
The high Lama
gathers his robes
across his shoulders
And casts his solemn
eyes,
The lecture
is full about
emptiness,
Words woven
into awesome concepts,
Aggregates
of emotions deconstructed,
Parts of the chariot
taken apart,
wheel by wheel.

Thinking imagined;
a thought
without a thinker,
The self
appears
without itself,
I am nothing
therefore I am,
The incense smoke
twists and twirls,
Weaving itself
over
the Buddha statue.

Prahlad Shekhawat

In the haze of smoke,
ritual words
and profound sound
abounds.
Buddha's equanimity
appears
as smiling or?
depending
on the angle of one's view

The Church in the Wilderness

The church
in the wilderness
is nestled
in the pine trees
and
wild growth,
Big cracks
in the wall witness
from
the earthquake
at the century's beginning,
Wrecking plans
for the British Raj's
future summer capital.

The cemetery
contains epitaphs
like
death due to snake bit
or dysentery,
or perhaps what seems as
another such illness
like Raj fatigue.
The wilderness
around the church
holds another communion,
white mountain goats
graze around
the tomb stones,

Prahlad Shekhawat

red faced monkeys
leap around
climbing drain pipes,
A brown snake
is bending to blend
with
the curving grass,
In the cracks
of the church walls,
in Gods
abandoned house corner,
A pipal tree
has found
it's natural habitat.

Prahlad Shekhawat

Traveller

Travelling
from one destination
to another
Only
upon arrival
one finds
what was lost,
what
was left behind
and what was
worth carrying.

After many journeys
the weight of the past
baggage
is lighter,
It is easier
to leave
left luggage,
to leave
the extra blanket
for the needy
to pick up.
What
was precious to carry
is a burden now,
Belongings
that
do not belong,

Prahlad Shekhawat

only
bare necessities
survive,
an explorer's
curious mind
makes up the rest,
Stripped
of prejudices
and judgments
one
becomes
a mere traveller,
so that one can
or as the poet Tagore said:
'Scatter the riches
one gathers
on the road'

Prahlad Shekhawat

Mind's Breath Travelling

Look the cloud
is moving
Or the wind
is moving,
The mind moving
with it
Look
the meditator's belly
is moving

Or is it
the breath moving
and
the mind's attention
moving the breath
Is it breath attention
moving
Moving up and down
knowingly
Is the mind
Moving
with the breath

Or the breath
moving with mind
Either way
knowingly or unknowingly
Up, down---up, down
Until the breather
and the breath
become
one.

Wandering with the Breath

Stillness
between inhaling
and exhaling
can trigger old
troubling emotions
In new presences
create space
to be one
with breathing
To flow
with the varying
breathing rhythms

Hearing
the heart beat faintly
in stillness
as a
percussion
to body's silent orchestra
I can hear the swift wind
breathing
through the valley
like my
wandering attention

The winds
wandering breath
mingles in between
light and darkness
The mountain and wind
become one
One with
one's expanding self
and nature self
the egoself becoming
the ecoself.

Prahlad Shekhawat

Window Tree

I look far
through my window tree
At the changing
hues and moods
of the sky
At times pale
water colour,
shady, stormy
perhaps still undecided.
Too bright
and too perfect blue,
even through or
because of
my tinted glasses.

In a week or so,
the tree has come alive
with new divine greens,
From bare stumps
more extended branches
displaying shiny shoots.
In the dancing light,
an invisible,
yet audible Koyal
and other unknown
birds
bring movement,
more life to
the leaf flowering tree

Prahlad Shekhawat

Suddenly I can see
many small birds
jumping across
Growing curious
at their shades of colours,
designs, lineage,
Appearing at strange times
of the day from in transit
from where to where?
What mixed or
mixed up seasons,
or messages
mixed with my imagining,
do they carry?

Prahlad Shekhawat

Solitude and Loneliness

Me and my
empty loneliness
and full solitude
Why does it feel
In between
the two;
Loneliness and solitude
as if someone
is around
long enough
to build
on fleeting images
of hope.
Loneliness of crowds
In the city
and solitude
of the quiet valley
that begins to expand one
free
but fear of
aloneness engulfs
Yet nature; like the
one friendly
surrounds one
like someone is around
filling with hope,
drop by drop
one's glass of hope.

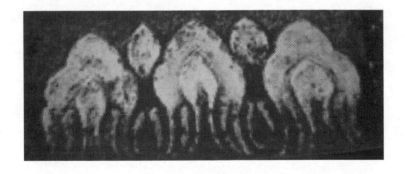

Prahlad Shekhawat

Fellow Traveller

My fellow traveller
and old friend
My second self
how are you doing
how is the spirit
and its movement
Send some emotion
worth remembering
Maybe I too can wield
my rhythm pen
to make it into a poem,
Perhaps an idea
of misery may become
a tale of hope.
an out of tune sadness
may become
a more profound poem.
You forgot me
but at least
for the sake of
the honour of
our half finished poem,
send an emotion or idea
so that one can
gather broken half sentences
and make them into
a full poem.

Two birds and Joy

The strange
selfless feeling
of joy
Watching the others
Skilful and doing well.
Buddha called it
affirming
from
a higher position
of
sympathetic joy
in
other's
doing well,

The mind readers of today
or psychologists
have discovered
a new emotion,
as new as
the beginning
of humanity.
Another way of
Being
and becoming
When the heart
is emptied
of envy
and jealousy
like watching
a couple in love,

absorbed
in each other,
perhaps revelling
In nothing more
than sweet nothings.
On the bough
of the pippla tree sit two birds
One
eats the fruit,
the other watches
Asks a Hindu holy book:
both are happy;
which is
happier?

Prahlad Shekhawat

No Message is Found

Whenever
the heart
feels
longing
A
familiar friendly
reminder
sound,
The wind
whispers,
breeze
cools
and
birds sing.
Smoke rises
from
nowhere
distance,
No message
is found
Yet
somehow
one
waits
around

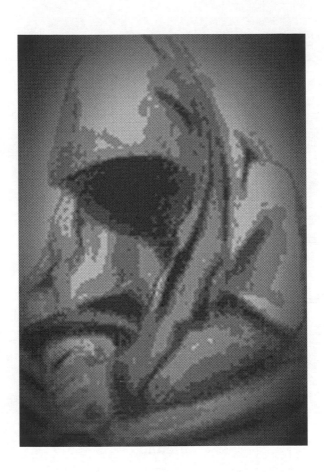

Prahlad Shekhawat

A Beggar Woman's Blessings

Besides the temple,
near
the golden statues,
smelling of incense
and flowers
I go to
that street corner
where
a leper women
huddles
in the rain
above
the smelly drain.

sometime
she
gives me
blessings
sometimes
I give her
a blanket,
Some worry
it maybe a strange
exchange,
I feel
it is maybe
more than
a fair
exchange.

Who knows
the mystery
of a
beggar women's
blessings
may carry
it's own
mystical power,
surpassing
a high Lama's
or a Guru's
holy blessings
and more power
than
any rates
of exchange.

An American Nun friend

I sort of dated
an American
Buddhist lady
She was
ordinary,
clean,
a little
too sincere.
She was
debating
to become
a Nun.
Yes becoming
a nun
can be
in a way
more
or less
than
a Buddhist.
I may have
become
her boy friend
and saved her,
or she

may have
saved me,
Or I may have
nudged her
to shave
her head.
I could have
Given
Her a choice,
if I could
first choose
myself.
She had gone
so far
ahead,
what point in
wooing her.
Could it be
achievement
of overcoming
a challenge
To help her
moderate,
wearing
holy clothes
under a bare head
Is not mandatory
to find
the awakening

the middle path.
I hesitated,
Almost
giving up.
When I
found myself
in love
I found her
in the monastery
Her hands
folded,
her eyes
down cast,
the time was
past.
A nun has little
patience
and less
compassion
for a man,
who waits
too long
to ponder
about
strange lives,
and how
to care
for
them.

Prahlad Shekhawat

Holy and Romantic Man

A cloud full of
mixed colour
Contains
half
soothing rain
and half
stormy hail
A half
holy
and half
romanitc man
makes the drama
of Dharma
full.

Prahlad Shekhawat

A Romantic Holy Man

King in Palace
up high
A poet of wine
and women
in tavern below.
A romantic man,
whose melodies
fine tune
to balance
Palace
in the clouds
built on
earth,
women
and
Jugs of wine.

Prahlad Shekhawat

Too Much Snow &
Too Little Water

Never seen so much snow
on the mountains,
I shivered going up
the valley
in the shimmering view,
Last year the snow
it was too little too late.

The woman in village
had to cut wheat
half ripe,
Not knowing
when
to plant the corn
next.
Cyber cafe boy
puzzled over
the frequent power cuts,
The storming power cables
still down.

Tourists revelling
in the dancing light,
swinging wild wind,
Do not have to wait
for the monsoons
to watch the show;
the 'son et lumaire'
of thunder,
Of the often
random changing
weather or season,
Who can tell
Some can.

Prahlad Shekhawat

Mountain Witness

king of the earth,
Wearing a white crown
and a green coat
Its deep valley holds
the bends in the rivers,
Sprouting springs,
channelling winds
in mysterious currents.
The mountains gather
to grow
ramblings of Lava,
Form the bosom
of the earth,
Abode of Shiva;
the divine energy
since beginning of time,
Preserver of forests,
its creatures
and the wilderness
which wrap around the mountain
the son of wind,
Ferrying Himalayan
medicinal herbs.

The mountain rocks
have seen civilisations come and go,
Melting like the snow
into the clear streams,
Mix with earth
plastic and urine.
They hold vigil long
after many cultures;
The Gaddi nomadic tribes,
the Pahadi tradesman
The Tibetan Buddhists
and the Western seekers,
have stretched
and exhausted themselves,
ever renewing,
flowing
or drowning in dry dust.
From further North
over the ice passes,
Another tradesman
is waiting to descend.

Those from
the Lhasa plateau,
with their frozen spirit,
Being pushed South
for unfreezing
warm reform.
Where wills this push
and shove,
These tectonic shifts
under the earth's surface.
Into the Kangra Valley,
skirting
a troubled neighbour,
Where will it end?
No messenger signals
to the mountains,
they somehow know,
where the wind
is sort of blowing.
The whispering breeze
and the singing birds
Alert them
to a half known future

Prahlad Shekhawat

My India

From my window
I can see
the first rays
kiss the ground,
The Pahadi landlady
is ready with flowers,
incense
and a pot of water
pouring with prayers,
The most powerful Gayatri Matnra
is a salute
to the Sun God,
Later on the way
I see the remains;
flowers, rice
in cow dung circles,
Dhup smoke still floating
with its smell
of familiar Indianness,
A red faced monkey
at the edge
of the playing ground,
greets me
with a quizzical glance,
near the half burnt
waste dump.

On the gentle path
up the hill
to my restaurant,
School children
with heavy bags
and light determined steps,
tourists clutching yoga mats
and mineral water bottles,
pass me by.
Suddenly I recognise
Myself
in the school boy's face.
A whiff of
pine flavoured aromain
my nostrils
through which
I had meditated mindfully.
inhaling
and exhaling 'prana'
The transformer comes alive
with exploding
crackling fireworks,
The poles
from the storm
some days ago
are still down,
The wires hanging
like Yama's sword (sword of the deity death)

The construction work
never ends,
bang bang
becomes a drone,
Punctuated
by papiha
and koyal bird songs.
The loud mother
and sister in law
serials,
burst through
my head phones.
A bird flies randomly,
smoke rises
in the distant sky
Nearby
a charas (marijuana) joint is lit,
Making a dent
in the unfolding
mysteries of awareness.
This is my India,
its sounds
and smells,
Mind enhancing,
mind boggling,
Never dull
or moderate.

Printed in the United States
By Bookmasters